REFINED INTERIORS

RIZZOLI
NEW YORK
New York Paris London Milan

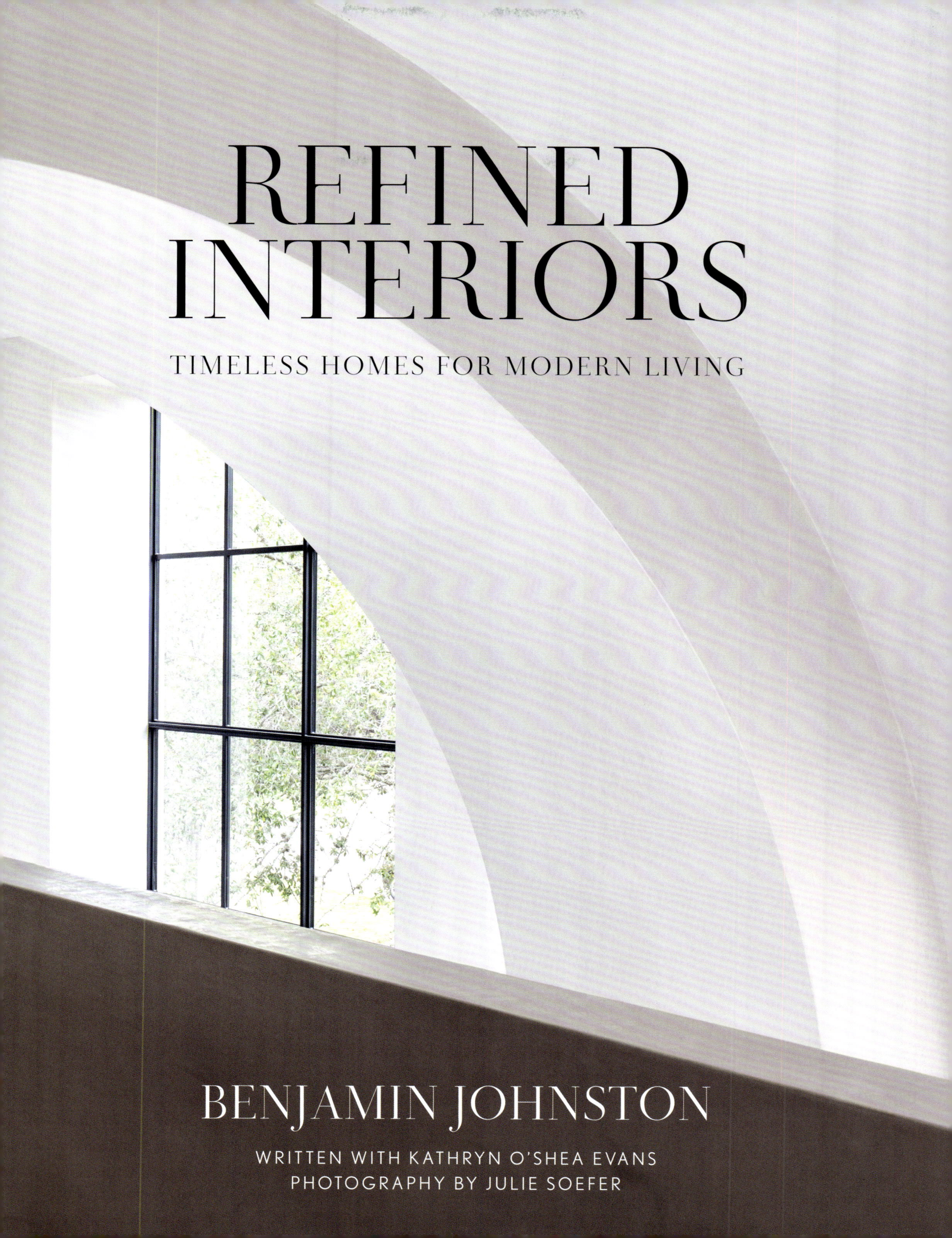

REFINED INTERIORS

TIMELESS HOMES FOR MODERN LIVING

BENJAMIN JOHNSTON

WRITTEN WITH KATHRYN O'SHEA EVANS
PHOTOGRAPHY BY JULIE SOEFER

To all the dreamers who create beauty in the world.
You inspire me.

James Castle
Memory Palace
at 100
SCOTT MITCHELL HOUSES
STUDIO KO

Contents

Introduction

I was raised with the belief that opportunity was something you could create. My mother often quoted television icon Milton Berle: "If opportunity doesn't knock, build a door." That idea, along with her unwavering faith that failure does not truly exist—only lessons—shaped the way I see the world. Those were not just words. They were values I absorbed deeply. They became instinct. They became faith.

From an early age, I trusted myself to make choices without overthinking them. I believed that every decision—right or wrong—would eventually lead to wisdom. That mindset carried me forward with quiet confidence: I didn't fear missteps. I welcomed them as part of growing up.

That same instinct guided me to St. John's, a competitive preparatory school in Houston. A scholarship made it possible for me to attend, and the experience opened my world vastly. At St. John's I was introduced to art, architecture, and theater—and perhaps most formatively, to the homes of classmates whose families had worked with architects and interior designers. I absorbed those spaces, aware even then that something meaningful happened when design was done with intention and care.

I was not the top student, but I was endlessly curious. I learned how to stretch myself. I built theater sets, performed on stage to overcome my fear of public speaking and a stutter, and began to see design not just as an academic pursuit, but as a tool for growth and self-expression.

As high school graduation neared, I applied to Texas A&M for architecture. The decision to target only one school might have caused anxiety for some, but I didn't second-guess it and felt fortunate to be admitted. Later, I continued with graduate studies at the University of Texas at Austin, following the same intuitive approach: do what feels right, and trust the rest to unfold.

My first professional opportunity came in Tokyo, working in the satellite office of the renowned architect César Pelli. I dove into large-scale commercial projects, which were dynamic and exciting. But something was missing. I realized that I desired to work on projects that felt more human-scale, tactile, and personal.

So with a grateful heart and a curious mind, I came home in search of new adventures. Back in Houston, I didn't have a firm plan. I simply started. I hung up my design shingle and offered my skills to anyone who needed them. From small bathroom remodels to furniture and graphic design for local restaurants, I said yes to anything that inspired me creatively. Over time, I began to see the shape of my career more clearly. Without meaning to, I had become an interior designer. With that realization came focus, and I pursued larger projects that allowed me to hone my instincts and expand my abilities.

What I love most about this profession is how it sits at the intersection of so many forces: ancient tradition and modern technology, art and science, beauty and utility. It connects us to the past through craftsmanship and to the future through innovation. It supports local economies, uplifts communities, and allows us to tell deeply personal stories through the spaces we shape and inhabit. I'm endlessly inspired by the artists, builders, and visionaries I've worked with—people who bring soul to every stone, stitch, and stroke of color. And I feel lucky—so lucky—to spend my life doing something that helps people feel more at home, more seen, and more inspired.

As my experience deepened, so did my practice. My studio grew slowly and intentionally, as did our range of services—from interior design to full-scale architectural work. I was fortunate to collaborate with an amazing team, wonderful clients, and talented collaborators and craftspeople. My projects began to take me across North America, from New York to Los Angeles, from Canada to Mexico. Travel, architecture, people, and storytelling continue to inspire me.

I've dedicated my life to this pursuit: as a designer, artist, teacher, and tastemaker, always with one goal in mind—to bring beauty into the world and help others do the same. This book is a reflection of that journey. It's a visual archive of the places, people, and lessons that shaped my career and my process—and a celebration of the spaces that speak when design is done with heart, clarity, and the pursuit of excellence. In these pages, I hope to inspire you to bring beauty into your own life as I share some of the wonder that keeps me coming back to fill my cup at the font of creativity.

PRINCIPLES

ARCHITECTURE

Architecture and interior design are not separate disciplines but two interconnected forces. While interior design breathes personality and purpose into a home, architecture provides the structure. Great architecture is the canvas that allows interior design to truly come alive. The layout of spaces, the flow between rooms, and the placement of walls and windows orchestrate how light, air, and movement interact within a project. A well-conceived floor plan that maximizes natural light, frames captivating views, and balances openness with intimacy defines the building's character.

Architecture also plays a vital role in situating a home in its environment. Materials, proportions, and structural details create a sense of place. Whether the home is sleek and modern with minimalist lines or a traditional space adorned with intricate moldings, the architectural style sets the tone for the interior. These design choices ripple through every aspect of the home, influencing furniture, finishes, and color palettes to create a seamless connection between the exterior and interior.

Light and shadow are another dimension of architectural design that profoundly impacts interiors. Windows, skylights, and other openings are functional features that also craft atmosphere. A picture window transforms a stunning view into living art, while clerestory windows flood a room with soft, diffused light that enhances textures and colors.

Architectural details act as a sculptural backdrop for interior design, providing character and depth that furnishings alone cannot achieve. Vaulted ceilings, exposed beams, arched openings, and custom millwork contribute artistry and craftsmanship. These elements elevate the space, adding layers of interest and context. A beautifully designed fireplace or a dramatic staircase becomes a centerpiece, inviting interior design to respond in ways that complement and enhance.

Ultimately, architecture anchors and inspires interior design, providing the framework within which every detail finds its purpose. Together, they create a cohesive vision—a home that is not just functional or beautiful but an authentic expression of life and art. When architecture and design work in unison, they produce a space that feels timeless, meaningful, and alive.

PREVIOUS: Our sculptural staircase is an ode to dramatic restraint. It became an ideal backdrop for the homeowner's butterfly painting by Hunt Slonem. OPPOSITE: The oversized windows and arched ceilings provide drama in this home. An eclectic mix of antique and modern pieces in the foyer set the tone for the experience throughout. Layering in plants and greenery—such as this leggy ficus tree—brings the outdoors to the interior.

SCALE

Scale is one of the most essential elements in interior design. It is the key to creating harmony and balance. Scale isn't just about the size of an object; it's about its proportion, its relationship to its surroundings, and the way it influences how a space feels and functions. Scale makes design dynamic and expressive. It shapes how individual pieces relate to architecture and to one another.

The interplay of scale profoundly affects how we perceive a room. In a space with soaring ceilings, oversized furniture can ground the room, making it feel inviting and proportionate to its dimensions. In contrast, compact areas benefit from slimmer, more delicate pieces that maintain a sense of openness and functionality. The art lies in knowing when to push boundaries and when to adhere to proportionate relationships, ensuring that every choice enhances the room's purpose and character.

While traditional design rules—like choosing a light fixture based on room dimensions—can be useful, we go beyond rigid guidelines to embrace artistic intuition. For instance, a dramatic oversized chandelier in a modest dining room defies conventional wisdom, but it can deliver a bold statement that transforms the space.

Lighting is a perfect example of scale's transformative power. A thoughtfully chosen fixture does more than provide illumination—it becomes a sculptural element that defines the room's personality. In some cases, a large chandelier can elevate a simple space into something extraordinary, creating a focal point that commands attention. Alternatively, in rooms where the architecture or furnishings already take center stage, smaller-scale lighting provides a subtle yet effective touch. Achieving this balance requires a nuanced understanding of how each element interacts within the larger context of the design.

Scale is a thread that weaves through every aspect of a room, influencing its functionality, flow, and aesthetic impact. When handled with care, it creates a foundation of harmony that ensures the space feels cohesive and intentional. By starting with function, thoughtfully considering scale, and layering in decorative details, we craft interiors that are not only visually striking but also deeply livable and emotionally resonant.

When our clients longed for a light fixture that was playful and casual, we enlisted Volker Haug to design a visually kinetic installation that reads like a large, swirling vortex. Its scale balances the weight of the square table, custom-made to seat twelve dinner guests. Framed by linen sheer drapery and floor-to-ceiling steel windows, the room feels airy yet grounded.

INTENTION

A client and friend recently remarked that the spaces my firm creates feel distinctly intentional. Her comment struck a chord with me, because I believe at the core of our work lies a deep commitment to uncovering and designing what is essential—elements that are vital to a project's success. Designing with intention is more than a methodology; it is a guiding principle that shapes every choice we make, ensuring the spaces we create resonate on both functional and emotional levels.

Intention begins with functionality: how do our clients envision living within their spaces? Functionality is not merely about fulfilling basic needs; it's about enriching daily life. Is this a room where a family will gather to share meals and host vibrant conversations among friends? Or is it a sanctuary for quiet reflection and rejuvenation? We also consider the rhythms of time—how the space will be experienced at different times of the day or in each of the four seasons—and the moods it should inspire. These questions lay the groundwork for every design decision that follows.

Intentional design goes beyond creating visually appealing spaces. It is about crafting environments that feel deeply personal and purposeful. Every element—whether a bold architectural feature or a subtle accessory—is selected with care to ensure that it plays a meaningful role and contributes to the overall harmony of the space. By adhering to this principle, we create spaces that foster a profound sense of connection and belonging.

Ultimately, designing with intention is a journey of exploration and deliberate decision-making. It's a process of asking the right questions, remaining open to possibilities, and striking a balance between logic and creativity, structure and spontaneity. This approach allows us to design interiors and exteriors that are as functional as they are beautiful, as timeless as they are personal. Through this lens, our work becomes more than design—it becomes a reflection of the lives and aspirations of those who inhabit the spaces we create.

A celebration of bold contrast and curated color, this layered entry sequence intentionally leads the eye—and the imagination—through sculptural moments and collected works. Geometric tile provides a classic, elegant counterpoint to the more modern graphic art and lighting.

JUXTAPOSITION

Juxtaposition is a balancing act that infuses spaces with energy, character, and timeless appeal. It's the artful curation of contrasting elements—style, era, texture, or tone—that transforms a room from ordinary to captivating. By blending furnishings from different time periods, mixing styles, or contrasting interior design with the architectural framework, juxtaposition allows for the creation of unique narratives that reflect individuality, lifestyle, and artistic vision.

At its essence, juxtaposition works because contrast generates vitality: think of a streamlined sofa paired with an ornate antique table, or a minimalist interior complemented by vibrant, eclectic art. This tension between opposites adds depth and intrigue, and each piece amplifies the other's impact. Rather than letting any single style dominate, juxtaposition crafts a harmonious balance—a symphony of influences that captivates and engages.

Juxtaposition also invites the unexpected. Pairing contrasting textures—such as smooth marble with raw wood or soft velvet with industrial steel—creates tactile interest and adds layers of complexity. Bold patterns juxtaposed with calming neutrals or a striking contemporary sculpture placed among vintage furnishings also keep the interiors from feeling one-note.

This principle extends beyond furnishings to the interplay between architecture and interior design. Some of the most compelling spaces arise when interiors deliberately contrast with the architectural envelope. A sleek, minimalist interior within a historic building—or a contemporary addition to a traditional home—creates dialogue between the old and the new, the ornate and the understated. This artistic tension honors a space's history while injecting it with individuality and modern relevance.

Juxtaposition makes spaces feel alive. The beauty of contrasts reflects the multifaceted lives and interests of the inhabitants. These spaces don't just serve as functional rooms; they become conversation starters, evoking emotion and sparking curiosity.

When executed with care, juxtaposition transforms a house into an authentic expression of identity—a place where disparate elements come together in perfect harmony to create something wholly unique and utterly beautiful.

My own home's jewel-toned lounge epitomizes luxury with a wink. The brass coffee table with an inlay of sodalite and resin by Belgian designer Yann Dessauvages is one of my favorite elements. It cannot be styled; it's an art piece in itself, and it is the perfect foil for the Regency period chairs upholstered in Pierre Frey fabric.

AUTHENTIC DESIGN
THE LIVING ROOM
CABINET OF CURIOSITIES

THEATER

Designing is much like directing a play. Each space should have its stars, a dynamic supporting cast, and an immersive set that forms the backdrop for the drama of daily life. It's not just about arranging furniture—it's about curating a stage where life unfolds with elegance, purpose, and character.

At the center of this production are the stars of the room, the elements that command attention and set the tone. These might be a dramatic chandelier casting a golden glow, a velvet-clad sofa that invites people to sink in, or an iconic piece of art that draws everyone's gaze. Like a lead actor captivating an audience, such standout features anchor the space, shaping its mood and defining its narrative.

Supporting these stars are talented ensemble members: furnishings and accents that add depth and dimension to the story. Side tables, layered rugs, sculptural lamps, and inviting lounge chairs play these roles with grace; they provide texture, contrast, and functionality. They make the space feel layered and complete without overshadowing the main attraction.

The set design—the architectural framework of walls, floors, ceilings, and lighting—provides the context for the production. These foundational elements, not always obvious at first glance, create the mood and establish a sense of place, much like a theater set. Lighting, the most ephemeral element, shifts the atmosphere seamlessly: bright and invigorating for moments of energy, soft and intimate for quiet reflection. This architectural envelope creates the stage on which life's moments are played out, and it adapts beautifully to both day and night.

Ultimately, architecture and interior design are ever-evolving performances. As seasons change and lives progress, the set may shift, new characters may enter, and even the starring roles may be recast. But the goal remains constant: to create a space that inspires, comforts, and elevates—just like the most unforgettable productions on stage. The magic lies not in the individual elements but in how they work together.

We enlisted local craftsmen to create this dramatic, monolithic room divider and bar made of two-toned brass and inset walnut paneling. The waterfall bar surface was hewn from a live-edge slab of tree that was over five feet wide by twenty-five feet. The resulting room feels like a cocktail boîte-meets-art gallery, and all the materials sing in dramatic harmony.

IMPERFECTION

Perfection is rarely memorable. A space that is overly polished or meticulously curated often lacks soul. Every space benefits from a touch of the unconventional—something unexpected, imperfect, or even a little ugly. These moments of imperfection create tension, intrigue, and depth, disrupting predictability and ensuring the space feels dynamic and alive.

Embracing imperfection doesn't mean sacrificing beauty; rather, it means acknowledging that beauty can be found in the unexpected. Introducing a raw, unrefined, or slightly jarring element injects a spark of energy into a space. It's the interplay between the polished and the rugged, the sleek and the awkward, that gives a room its unique identity and makes it truly captivating.

Brutalist art and architecture serve as powerful inspiration for these moments of "ugly beauty." With its raw, unapologetic forms and unembellished materials, Brutalism celebrates imperfection and authenticity. A Brutalist sculpture, with its rough textures and commanding presence, can serve as a striking focal point that anchors a refined interior. Similarly, a Brutalist coffee table with organic shapes and unfinished edges grounds a space filled with soft fabrics and sleek finishes.

These imperfect elements do more than disrupt visual perfection; they bring balance. Design thrives on contrast, and without it, a room risks feeling too precious or delicate. A heavy, raw, or imperfect piece—a vintage chair with patina or a group of mismatched tiles, or an offbeat light fixture—acts as a grounding force within a carefully curated design. These pieces challenge the aesthetic status quo, becoming protagonists in the story of the space.

Beyond their visual impact, these elements tell a story. They contribute history and a sense of humanity. Unlike a flawless mass-produced item, an object with rough edges or visible marks of craftsmanship feels alive, authentic. This makes the surrounding space feel approachable and lived-in rather than untouchable or staged.

Ultimately, incorporating a little bit of ugly isn't about embracing flaws but about achieving balance. It's about designing spaces that are real, layered, and full of personality. These moments of imperfection remind us that design, like life, is most compelling when it surprises us.

This Brutalist-inspired, cast-bronze klismos chair was designed by Reagan Hayes. With organic, rough texture it is the definition of what I call "ugly beauty" and supplies the needed tension between plush and punch.

ART

Art is a powerful medium for storytelling. Whether working with a seasoned collector who has amassed an extensive gallery of pieces or a client just entering the art world, our goal is always the same: to integrate art so that it is visually striking and feels personal. Art connects us to our humanity, and when thoughtfully incorporated into an interior, it elevates both the space and the lives of those who inhabit it.

For longtime collectors, our role often involves creating harmony between their cherished pieces and the interior design. Their collections already carry profound meaning, so the challenge lies in curating how they are displayed. A bold, abstract painting might become the centerpiece of a contemporary living room, while a delicate landscape could add serenity to a cozy bedroom. Sculptural works bring dimension and intrigue, serving as focal points that invite interaction and admiration. The goal is always to let the artwork shine while ensuring it feels seamlessly integrated into the design narrative.

When clients are new to collecting, the process is equally rewarding. Together, we embark on a journey of discovery, exploring pieces that resonate with them. In starting their collections, we encourage them to consider a diverse mix of media, from paintings and photography to sculpture and textiles.

Art evokes emotion and energy. A vibrant, colorful piece infuses a room with playfulness and dynamism, while a monochromatic work lends an air of sophistication and calm. The scale, placement, and framing are also key. A dramatic, oversized canvas can command attention as the star of a room; a thoughtfully curated gallery wall adds depth and intrigue, inviting viewers to linger.

By weaving art into the design process, I can craft interiors that are not just visually stunning but also deeply personal and meaningful. My passion for artwork stems from its transformative power. It turns a house into a home and a collection of rooms into a living gallery. When artwork is incorporated, the entire space comes alive, resonating with the individuality and spirit of those who call it home.

The traditional white-walled art gallery finds its rebuttal in this space, where a mixed media piece by Edoardo Giordano has an ideal backdrop in the moody, aubergine plaster walls upon which it hangs. After all, it was the artist's palette that inspired the colors used throughout the interior. As such the room becomes the perfect setting for twilight conversations—layered, luxe, and undone in all the right ways.

COLOR

Even in the most understated spaces, the eye craves contrast, vibrancy, and moments of inspiration. Color, whether bold and daring or soft and intentional, has the remarkable ability to transform interiors into spaces that inspire and reflect the unique personalities of those who live there.

Neutral interiors offer undeniable strengths: they provide a serene foundation and timeless appeal. However, without the infusion of color—a vibrant painting, an unexpected rug, or a playful accent—these spaces can feel flat and uninspired. The human eye naturally seeks contrast and variety, and even those drawn to neutrals often find themselves captivated by a well-placed pop of color, whether consciously or not.

For those willing to embrace color fully, the possibilities are endless. Color doesn't just enhance a room visually; it shapes its mood and atmosphere. Deep, saturated hues can energize and invigorate, while softer tones bring calm and comfort. Color evokes emotion, making it a powerful tool for tailoring interiors to align with the lives and aspirations of their inhabitants.

The use of color in design is deeply personal. It's not about applying color indiscriminately but about incorporating it thoughtfully to create spaces that are as unique as the people who call them home. In a home with spaces that must serve in a number of different ways, color can also serve to define and balance different areas and moods. I like to approach the design of rooms by defining when they are to expected to serve most optimally: daytime, nighttime, or both. A vibrant living room with bold artwork and eye-catching furniture fosters energy and inspiration, while a tranquil bedroom in muted, soothing tones becomes a sanctuary of rest. These carefully curated shifts in palette within the same home create a dynamic, layered environment that supports a variety of emotions, tasks and experiences.

Ultimately, designing with color is about celebrating individuality and bringing spaces to life. Whether through daring choices or subtle accents, color provides the vibrancy and personality that make an interior feel complete—turning a home from simply a collection of rooms into a choreographed reflection of those who live within.

For a dining experience drenched in drama, we wrapped this room in verdant olive plaster, then echoed the tone in the dining chairs. Bold abstract art provides polychromatic energy, while the symmetry of the other elements—a sculptural chandelier and inky black urns—grounds the palette.

TEXTURE

Texture is the unsung hero of interior design—a subtle yet transformative element that adds depth, warmth, and character to a space. While color and form often grab the spotlight, texture works quietly in the background, connecting what we see to what we feel. From the soft plushness of a rug to the cool smoothness of marble, texture engages the senses and transforms interiors from merely attractive to deeply resonant.

In furnishings, incorporating texture begins with the choice of materials. A velvet sofa exudes comfort and luxury, while a linen armchair offers understated elegance. An earthy jute rug grounds a room, while a silk throw introduces a touch of indulgence. The key to unlocking texture's potential lies in layering: pairing contrasting elements like rough with smooth, soft with hard, and matte with glossy creates a dynamic experience. Without this variety, a space risks feeling flat—uniformly sleek or overwhelmingly coarse.

Texture isn't limited to furnishings; it's deeply embedded in the architecture of a space. Elements like exposed wooden beams, raw brick walls, or intricate moldings add authenticity and character, anchoring the design with a sense of history and permanence. Meanwhile, polished concrete floors or smooth plaster walls provide a sleek, contemporary counterbalance. Even the smallest architectural details—such as brushed metal hardware—contribute to the sensory tapestry. These textures not only enrich the design but also lay a foundation for softer elements within the space.

One of texture's greatest strengths is its ability to evoke sensory moments that engage both the eyes and the hands. Indeed, texture is a powerful emotional tool, because it turns a space into an experience. A space layered with textures draws the eye to explore its nuances and invites touch to appreciate its contrasts. Imagine the satisfying feel of running your fingers along a leather-wrapped banister or tracing the raised patterns of grasscloth wallpaper. These tactile interactions add intimacy and set the mood. Natural, irregular materials like wood and stone make a space feel welcoming and organic. In contrast, smooth surfaces like glass and lacquer convey sophistication and modernity. Texture, in its quiet yet transformative way, brings a space alive with sensory delight.

This sitting area is a study in tactile elegance; plush bouclé, a shaggy rug, and rich woods combine in a sensory symphony. Muted pinks and charcoal grays mingle like shadows at dusk. Above, the light fixture hovers like a carefully balanced mobile, against the pargework ceiling.

HOUSES

Organic Modernism

Architecturally speaking, the English Tudor period was not known for its airy lightness and soft modern interiors—quite the opposite, in fact. So when clients longed to bring a layered modern sensibility to house plans for a Tudor Revival design, we were initially dubious.

The existing architectural plans included gabled, pitched ceilings with lots of sharp angles and lines. We became excited by the notion and the challenge of resculpting the design into an organic modern symphony of curves—extensively on the interior, and more minimally on the exterior.

We took advantage of the epic sight lines that stretched through the dining room, entry, and stair hall and reimagined them into a vaulted sequence, illuminated by monumental steel and glass windows, that has an almost monastic quality. The resulting aesthetic is pared back and controlled, yet exalted and sculptural, with its curved ceiling, catwalk, and plaster walls. In general, I love the subtle undulations and mottling of plaster as a wall treatment; these plaster walls are made of marble dust and pigment that was first trawled on and then burnished. The result is walls that glimmer in the light and are a joy to touch.

One of the hallmarks of our reimagined interior is a curving staircase that nods to Frank Lloyd Wright's Guggenheim Museum thanks to its continuously flowing, spiral ascent. Echoing it on the other side, we reimagined the wine room as a showcase for their bottle collection, viewed through the curved glass wall that is the stairway's counterpart. Throughout the home, arcs and radiused corners became motifs that balanced the more rigid elements found in the architecture. For example, originally, the study was supposed to be very squared-off, with Old World ceiling beams. We introduced a curved cove around the exterior perimeter. Since we had done ivory-colored

PREVIOUS: Vestiges of the home's Tudor inspiration can be seen in the roof line and buttress detail seen in the front facade. OPPOSITE: Originally intended to be a Tudor-inspired grand hall, we re-envisioned it as a modern, organic space with soaring ceilings and walls softened with subtly shimmering plaster. In lieu of a window into the wine room, we designed an oenophile's showcase with glass panels that follow the swooping curve of the balcony above. FOLLOWING: We paneled the dining room wall with antiqued mirror to reflect the light coming through the monumental windows opposite.

THE ELEGANT LIFE
BEACHSIDE

plaster in much of the rest of the house, we wanted to explore a chromatic approach in the study. An artisan created a moody shade of plum that serves as the impetus for the room's palette—an enveloping backdrop that feels both intellectual and warm.

Curating and juxtaposing elements from various design epochs is a key method that can be used to suspend a home in time, and to make sure it doesn't feel locked into a particular day and age. With a wide-ranging approach to curation of furniture and furnishings, we incorporated midcentury and contemporary pieces with antiques more than one hundred years old. The results are magnetic, and as a whole the composition defies categorization.

We find that it's essential to include a bit of imperfection in every room. In this dining room, the rug we selected has a linear striped pattern, but rather than those stripes repeating straight across, there are places where the frequency is off. The stripes visually peel away in an intentionally disruptive manner for memorable effect. We also believe in incorporating elements that are a bit odd or even ugly. Take the vessels from Robert F. Lyon on the dining tabletop, which are sculpted from turned wood, horsehair tassels, pencils, and cork. Their oddness creates dynamic tension as they play with the rest of the space.

We also love challenging traditional color palettes. The mix of ochre, yellow, olive green, and orange you see in the family room is unconventional to say the least. The blend of rust, baby blue, brown, and charcoal we employed in the game room could be discordant. The primary bedroom features apricot, ochre, blue-green, and lavender. These colors together can be difficult to harmonize, but when they are purposely combined, magic happens. You can always make a color work by using at least one of two strategies. The aforementioned spaces all utilize the first: repeat a color at least once in a space, so that no single color stands alone. The other strategy we employ is to add the predominant color's complement in some equally powerful measure. For instance, if you have an all-purple room, then pull in a yellow accent with the flowers, as we did in the study. Either way, we want the colors to play off each other and create a dialogue. That is, in the end, what design is all about.

OPPOSITE: A vintage geometric painting by John Hiigli entitled *The Holy Grail* adds to the monastic feel of this dining space, while the graphic rug by Elte with its intentional imperfections and the sculptural horsehair vessels by Robert F. Lyon prove that "ugly" can be exquisite. Without a natural place to hang a chandelier, we commissioned Riloh to create an armature of our design to cantilever pendants over the table. FOLLOWING LEFT: A quiet moment in the family room, where sculptural florals and textured glazes nod to the home's earthy palette. FOLLOWING RIGHT: The mantel we designed is reminiscent of poured concrete blocks that echo the barrel-vaulted ceiling we added to the space.

BUNGALOW DETAILS: EXTERIOR
EVOCATIVE STYLE

RIGHT: The vaulted ceiling in the family room commanded design choices to suit the scale. We installed a light fixture that's seven feet in diameter, as well as a sculptural sofa that spans eighteen feet in length. Anything smaller would have felt wrong. FOLLOWING: The lines in the kitchen are crisp, but the mood is warm. Every decision, from the gray plaster finish on the vent hood that echoes the fireplace opposite in the family room to the cream-colored plaster walls, speaks to quiet, casual style.

WOLF

ABOVE: We loved the notion of adding a coffee and tea bar to the kitchen—a place to begin or end the day. Tailored, pleated café curtains supply coziness. OPPOSITE: The countertop backsplashes feature a scalloped treatment—a quarter-round moment that pops up throughout this home for approachable elegance. FOLLOWING: We introduced the curved cove around the perimeter of this office ceiling to soften the room's strong geometries. We took a chromatic approach to the walls by mixing marble dust with aubergine pigment.

ABOVE: In a home devoted to juxtaposition, this corner captures it all: masculine built-ins, a velvet sofa, and a commanding portrait whose subject is dressed in lipstick red. OPPOSITE: The fireplace hearth is intentionally asymmetrical, emphasizing curated imperfection and artistic tension.

RIGHT: There is power in small, sculptural things: playful handmade vessels and exaggerated textures make a house feel alive. In this home, we married 1970s quirkiness with contemporary refinement. FOLLOWING: Designed as a softly glowing counterpart to the main entertaining spaces, this bar lounge balances sculptural forms with golden-metal tones: brass and a deep bronze. PAGES 54-6: A hotel room in Orvieto, Italy, that was awash in traditional Roman colors inspired the color blocking in this primary bedroom. A vaulted plaster ceiling echoes the home's curvaceous ethos, while a series of custom Josef Albers–inspired studies bring the apricot palette to life. PAGE 57: Soft drapery and rounded seating complete the primary suite's balanced mix of elegance and ease. PAGES 58-9: The primary bathroom's silver travertine and softly curving architectural gestures turn this utilitarian space into a sanctuary.

THE LIVING ROOM

ROOM
by the Design Leadership Network
THE LIVING ROOM
ASSOULINE

NOMA
WORKSTEAD

ABOVE: Designed for lingering conversations over aperitifs, the alfresco space blends high design with high value and incorporates plenty of linen finishes for earthy softness. OPPOSITE: An organically shaped cocktail table anchors this covered terrace, where modern upholstery and timeless sculptural forms combine.

Regency Remix

I believe in being what I call a "universal designer," by which I mean a designer who is truly adaptable. Like an actor, a designer is a storyteller who channels the stories of other people. But in your own home, *you* and your loved ones are the story—after all, you're living out scenes there, day by day, memory by memory. So, I often tell my team that your own home should be a de facto design laboratory: a place to tinker with ideas and toil tirelessly with your own design DNA, challenging yourself to do new things without any radio feedback. It's one of the few places where you can express yourself in a wholly authentic way.

When my partner and I were building our own home from the ground up in a historic area of Houston, we took it as our opportunity to do just that. I knew from the start I wanted to channel the design periods that speak to me the most. The neoclassical golden age of the late 1800s through early 1900s is particularly inspirational to me, as it creatively confronted the Industrial Revolution. Roughly thirty years later came the Art Deco and Art Moderne movements, in which designers sculpted neoclassical forms into fresh, streamlined silhouettes. And then another thirty years after that, those same influences were reinterpreted through a cinematic lens with the Hollywood Regency style of the 1930s and 1940s. I took each era as an inspiration, selecting certain thematic elements that I wanted to incorporate into our own home. Those included slender columns from Hollywood Regency; streamlined fluting for the walls and custom marble mantel we designed and had hand-carved in Spain; and starburst motifs from the Art Deco and neoclassical periods. A few moments of materiality, such as the graphic use of contrasting marble in the mosaic floors, countertops, backsplashes, and other architectural elements, also repeat throughout.

OPPOSITE: The neoclassical fluting in our entryway gives texture and depth to the wall leading up to the plaster cove. The pairing of an églomisé and bright bronze entry table and a chandelier from Galerie Glustin delivers an unforgettable first impression—part Hollywood, part haute history. Classic herringbone wood floors ground the glamour. FOLLOWING: The lounge's architectural paneling and a modillion cornice provide a neoclassical backdrop for vibrant colors and contemporary decor. Gilded Regency period chairs are paired with a modern curved sofa and vintage Donghia seating. Layered on top of one of my rug designs for Madison Lily Rugs is a handcrafted brass and sodalite table by Belgian designer Yann Dessauvages.

A study in curated exuberance, our after-hours lounge celebrates repetition and rhythm. The fluted motif around the fireplace echoes the architecture elsewhere in our home, while vibrant modern art nods to my own fascination with color. The dramatic sconces are Stilnovo reproductions and they were carefully worked into the room's paneling. Notes of blackened brass and Lucite break up the rich color palette.

The movement of the sun's light was an unofficial muse, and we capitalized on it with a Victorian-style layout that flows around a central atrium. Philosophically, I feel that there are daytime rooms and evening ones, something we emphasized here. For rooms that I envisioned being experienced in the evening, we went a little darker, moodier, and more handsome. Our lounge, dining room, bedrooms, and powder room all fall into this category. Those spaces where we spend daytime hours were appropriately made brighter to capitalize on daylight. You'll notice our main living room toes the line between both; because we use it at all hours, we wanted it to be light and bright, but not without a punch of drama. We used the bright vermillion and lavender tones in a massive painting by Alex Couwenberg that hangs on one wall to inform our color palette. We filled the space with a mix of new and old furnishings with artistic statements, such as a solid bronze chair by Reagan Hayes. I call it a "specimen chair"; it's a bit Brutalist in its lines, and intentionally awkward. It's really meant to disrupt the room and keep it from feeling too buttoned up and pretty. Incidentally, the chair also weighs a ton. If there's ever a tornado here, I'm going to hide under that chair and hold on for dear life!

We wanted every single element of this house to feel special and be exquisitely crafted, so we enlisted the help of an amazing contractor and dear friend, Erin Stetzer, who brought excellent tradespeople to the table to carry out our vision. They worked tirelessly to get even the smallest details right. It was fun to encourage the whole team to stretch creatively, and the results were worth it. One room that shocks people is the primary bathroom, which is so graphic it looks like it could have been imagined in a fever dream of product designer Piero Fornasetti, or the surrealist artist Pedro Friedeberg. When friends or clients are touring our home, I'll often keep the pocket doors to that space closed, so it can enjoy a big reveal. When those doors slide open, jaws literally drop. While it is technically a classic white bathroom, its graphic use of tile and lighting make it anything but conventional.

As you move throughout our home, those thematic elements that we intentionally repeated have a certain pentameter, a certain rhythm—just as in poetry or songwriting. That creative thread runs from top to bottom, in daytime rooms and those for enjoyment after the sun sets. The story being told is all our own, and it is recounted proudly in our unique voice.

OPPOSITE: In a corner of the dining room, a sinuous brass console by Pietro Franceschini, sconce by Galerie Glustin, and vintage finds create artistic tension together.
FOLLOWING: Moiré silk by Dedar envelops our dining room, allowing the colorful art by Eric Sall to pop. Above the dining table and chairs I designed for Chaddock hangs an alabaster light installation made by Atelier Alain Ellouz.

MERT ALAS & MARCUS PIGGOTT

PREVIOUS: The altar-like Nero Marquina kitchen island glows in the evening hours with concealed lighting and seems to float above its fluted base. LEFT, TOP: A Murano glass reproduction chandelier adorns the ceiling in our kitchen. LEFT, BOTTOM: A painting by Tommy Fitzpatrick and Brutalist candlesticks add a personal touch. OPPOSITE: We enlisted a local metal artisan to wrap the upper cabinets in brass, then burnish and lacquer them for a rich effect.

RIGHT: Inky black walls and cabinets and warm brass hardware play off the black-and-white cubist tile underfoot in the catering kitchen. FOLLOWING: We wanted the main living room to be light and bright, but not overly color-saturated. Distributing hues from a vermillion and lavender painting by Alex Couwenberg throughout the space, via my furniture designs for Chaddock and my rug design for Madison Lily, ultimately created a room that feels casual, but delivers on drama as well.

WOLF
WOLF

INSIDE MILAN
NEW YORK
HEAVENLY BODIES

ART DECO
INSPIRED DESIGN

ABOVE: In our atrium, we repeated the fluting from the entryway in two additional sizes—a variation on the theme. OPPOSITE: The gallery wall of Rodney Smith photography draws the eye beyond the dynamic railing with its commanding presence.

Our modern interpretation of a modillion cornice appears throughout the home, including in the primary bedroom. Everything is crisply tailored here—a nod to men's suiting—but not stale, thanks to the curated tension that arises from notes of contrast, such as the convex mirror and tiger-print throw pillows.

INTERIOR AFFAIRS
HELMUT NEWTON
CLASSICISM AT HOME

OPPOSITE: Custom drapery with a rhythmic pattern provides a jolt of energy to this bedroom. ABOVE: A piece by Shozo Nagano contrasts the faceted black credenza beautifully. FOLLOWING: Our en suite bathroom is one of the most deliciously "extra" spaces in our homes. Custom marble inlay floors zigzag through the jewel box, which is crowned by a massive Murano glass chandelier.

We mirrored the saturated midnight blue of our primary bedroom in our wardrobe. I don't love the visual clutter of seeing everyone's belongings, so custom-designed wardrobes conceal the contents in the open-concept closet. Meanwhile, the hardware and light fixtures lend glamorous sparkle.

Men Without Ties
CALVIN KLEIN

INTERIOR DESIGN REVIEW

ABOVE AND OPPOSITE: Inspired by the iconic 1958 film *Auntie Mame*, our guest bedroom takes its cue from the 1920s modern set by art director Malcolm Bert. It features a palette of robin's egg blue, crisp white, and purple in every key—eggplant mohair, plum silk, and soft lavender underfoot. I designed the chairs and the bed for Chaddock; the latter is the world's first eight-poster bed and a modern nod to Palladian columns.

PREVIOUS: Like a pop-art vignette, our library of art books is a fever dream inspired, like the primary bath, by the works of Pedro Friedeberg and Piero Fornasetti. RIGHT: Neoclassical design was a major inspiration for the brick coursing on our home's exterior, while the slender columns were pulled directly from Hollywood Regency. The turf edging our pool is the definition of form and function: it hides French drains that offer maximum efficiency during the many Gulf Coast monsoons.

GRAY MALIN

Resort in Residence

If you have ever checked into a luxury resort and then been reluctant to leave, you may want to take a page from our clients' playbook. When this young family hired us to design the interiors of their new home—an expansive single story that sprawls sixteen-thousand square feet with soaring ceilings—one of their few requests was that it become a kind of resort, with all the amenities one might expect from a five-star hotel.

So, rather than hewing to the residential as a reference, we looked to commercial interiors to find ways to bring the voluminous spaces down to scale. Often, people are surprised to hear that extremely large rooms can be a design challenge, but it's true—especially if you want interiors that are approachable and livable. The ceilings throughout this home soar anywhere from twelve to twenty-two feet. To bring everything into focus, we created custom pieces that would balance the scale. For example, in the entry, forty-two-inch-tall sconces and a sculpture measuring eighty-four inches tall were employed. Had we chosen anything smaller, the space wouldn't feel balanced.

In the primary bedroom, we designed a dramatic headboard wall that is set in a niche and made of leather and stained oak paneling. This architectural device is more commonly seen in fine hotels than in residences, and it helps modulate the scale of the room, where the ceiling is a staggering fourteen feet high. If we had gone for a standard headboard, it would have felt miniscule, like a piece of dollhouse furniture. The nightstands are similarly oversized at forty-four inches wide. More conventionally sized nightstands would have looked under scale, leaving lots of space

OPPOSITE: To bring the entryway's soaring fourteen-foot ceilings down to a more human scale, we introduced large furnishings such as a seven-foot-tall sculpture, a three-and-a-half-foot-tall sconce, and a generously proportioned custom bench. Anything smaller in this space would have looked like dollhouse furniture; this trick of the eye allows the home to feel grounded.

between the bed and the corners of the room. Even the chandelier is a trick of scale: we reached out to its maker, Studio Endo, and commissioned a triple-tier version of their design to fill some of the vertical space in the room. There are technological thrills you might find in a hotel suite here, too, including cove lighting and automated draperies that open and close at the push of a button from the comfort of the bed.

As any hotelier can attest, sometimes you must get creative with materials to maximize impact. In many areas of this home, we gave materials a luxe effect by asking them to do more. In the media room, for example, we cut a grass cloth wallcovering from Phillip Jeffries into squares and rectangles and installed them to create a patchwork—rotating pieces so that the striations were turned different directions. In the laundry room, we employed three colors of porcelain tiles in a similarly unusual manner: we instructed the tile installer to slice them into various shapes that we used to create our own unique pattern. It's not something that exists anywhere else on earth. We invented it just for this project to make a statement: a graphic yet functional floor using unpretentious materials.

The vaulted living room is another example of reimagining things in unanticipated ways. We created our own light installation with varying styles of Volker Haug's existing pendant lights. We laid them out so they would drop and inhabit the space at different levels, allowing you to appreciate them from multiple perspectives as you move throughout the space or nestle in by the fireside for a cozy evening. Fitted with other artful choices—such as a goatskin lacquer and hammered-brass coffee table and a custom wool and silk rug—the room is exactly the type of grand space in which a resort guest might unwind at cocktail hour. The only thing missing is . . . room service?

OPPOSITE: With ceilings at twenty-two feet, the great room demanded a dramatic response. White oak paneling on the fireplace and white oak on the ceiling serve to visually break down what might otherwise have been a lackluster white box, while the custom installation of light fixtures from Volker Haug fills the airspace. During evening hours, these lights cast a lovely glow over the intimate seating arrangement below. FOLLOWING: Expansive steel windows frame the woods beyond the backyard oasis and create a seamless indoor/outdoor flow.

PIANO
West

TRUE WILDLIFE
VANITY FAIR 100 YEARS
PIANO
RANCHLAND
RALPH LAUREN A WAY OF LIVING
JOHN GALLIANO for DIOR

HEART AND HOME
ROOMS FOR LIVING
Interiors Atelier AM

PREVIOUS: The range hood in the kitchen is clad in corrugated blackened steel and trimmed in stainless, providing an unexpected accent. RIGHT: In the bar and wine room, wooden cabinets were clad in brass, then given patina and lacquered to lock in the muted finish. Textural finishes such as a metalized grasscloth, antique mirror on the ceiling, and the leathered finish on the Silver Wave marble countertops all shimmer at twilight as many sources of concealed architectural lighting begin to glow; the space is tailormade for a luxe cocktail hour experience.

LEFT TOP: The crackle finish of the pottery contrasts the lacquered parchment of the table, while the snake-skin patterned hide rug provides a delightful backdrop to both. LEFT BOTTOM: Lots of different textures combine in this upholstery moment. OPPOSITE: We refer to an arrangement of four chairs as a "quad pod"—a perfect setup for this family of four, who love to gather in the sitting area and reconnect over meaningful conversation. The oversized alabaster light fixture floats like a celestial moon above. FOLLOWING: Slabs of Mont Blanc quartzite in the kitchen echo the surface we used in the great room around the fireplace, providing a subtle thread of continuity.

100 YEARS OF BENTLEY
at 100

Good design lives in a careful balance—where utility meets beauty, where quietness finds character, and where the ordinary is energized by the unexpected.

OPPOSITE: This family longed for, in their words, "the prettiest chef's pantry ever," and we delivered. The rolling ladder adds charm and functionality. Though the materials are modest, the design and craftsmanship elevate this space.

EPICUREAN JOURNEYS

ABOVE: In the home office, custom dark-green shelving with inset brass strip details and shimmering grasscloth backing defines layered luxury. OPPOSITE: A wall of glass floods the space with natural light, balancing the drama of the dark bookcase wall behind the desk. FOLLOWING: To modulate the fourteen-foot ceilings in the primary suite, we niched in a headboard wall design of leather and wood panels. A standard headboard would have felt lost in such a large room.

GRAY MALIN

CALATRAVA

ART DECO
THE GRAND CANYON
GREAT ESCAPES EUROPE
VOGUE THE COVERS
art deco style
ROWDY MEADOW
BILLY COTTON

The primary bathroom channels spa-level luxury with double vanities in softly veined marble. The edge treatment gives the illusion of a much thicker profile. Dramatic lighting punctuates the space, while symmetry and serene materiality offer a timeless sense of retreat.

A suite of ultra-luxe touches—from integrated marble vanities to towering custom cabinetry that ups the feeling of grandeur—enhances the five-star feeling throughout the primary bath and dressing areas. Not shown: a dedicated washer/dryer and even a beverage fridge for hotel-level convenience, no butler required.

CHANEL

SKSA
BASEBALL
RIVER JOURNEYS

OPPOSITE: I believe children's rooms should be designed to grow with their occupants. For the son's room, we brought down the height of the twelve-foot ceilings by introducing Clarence House wallpaper on the inset ceiling and design elements that emphasize horizontality, including banded draperies and a headboard that spans the wall. ABOVE: We created a made-to-measure study nook with playful two-toned cabinetry and tack space.

RIGHT: A maximalist love letter to hue and texture, the daughter's suite was inspired by S. Harris drapery fabric with unapologetic flair. Sculptural upholstery and color drenching gave us results as radiant and multidimensional as the young lady herself. FOLLOWING: Crafted for alfresco entertaining, the outdoor kitchen pairs veined granite with warm wood cabinetry for a sleek, sculptural effect. PAGES 126–27: A putting green, sunken firepit, infinity edge hot tub, pool, and diving platform are just a few of the amenities we designed for the family's enjoyment.

FACE PAINT
Visions of Paradise
STRONG
SOFIA COPPOLA

Chang
Chang

Past Made Present

A longtime client of ours is a history obsessive with great taste; the last home that we meticulously restored and reinvented for her was one of the proud Federalist homes of Georgetown in Washington, D.C. When she called to tell us that she was buying a new home in Houston that was built in the early 2000s, we knew that we would be in for a challenge. That is not a vintage of architectural design known for classic sophistication. We decided that the goal was to make the house feel as if it had been there for two centuries, evolving over time.

Upon seeing the project, it struck us that everything felt heavy and dark, like a Tudor house that took a wrong turn through Tuscany and then had not been aired out in decades. None of it matched our client's aesthetic, but it had good bones and well-proportioned spaces. Of course, we would need to edit the existing architectural elements, while incorporating new ones to support or juxtapose against those that remained in place. We began by evicting the things that weren't doing the home any favors, like honey oak finishes, orange Saltillo tile, and beige walls. There was even a modern glass tube-elevator installed in the stairwell by a previous homeowner that simply had to go. Our goal was to freshen the architecture and lean into things that felt classic, while introducing elements from today. We kept the eyebrow arches, a groin-vault ceiling in the home's bar, and charming details like the acorn motif on the newel posts in the stairwell. Classic brown wood finishes were introduced with new wood flooring, and larger windows were incorporated to usher in more daylight.

One of our main design inspirations for the home was an English painting of a woman riding a horse that has been in the client's family for generations. This kicked off the home's color palette of rich, muted hues and helped hone our approach of Anglophile quiet luxury. The piece now hangs above the new Nero Marquina marble fireplace in the living room and looks like it was transported to Texas via a cottage in the Cotswolds. We are firm believers that every room needs a bit of black, and the new fireplace and its streamlined mantel of ebony marble not only ground the space but also help prevent the antique painting from reading as stuffy.

OPPOSITE: In the foyer flanked by eyebrow arches, we replaced an existing tile floor with inset wood herringbone. A horsehair trimmed stool by Konekt Studio is a modern nod to the pastoral English countryside. FOLLOWING: An heirloom family portrait inspired the home's palette and sense of place—equestrian meets Anglophile. The existing fireplace surround was reimagined in Nero Marquina marble, anchoring the new windows we installed to bring in more light.

INSPIRED DESIGN

Across from this intimate living room and the home's foyer is a lovely dining room. The entrance to the space is an eyebrow archway that we replicated along the dining room's back wall and layered with antique mirror to create an enfilade effect and to reflect more light. We enlisted a local artist to paint a mural on the walls that was meant to feel like an extension of the painting in the living room: an immersive take on the English countryside. There are misty fields punctuated by trodden pathways, and the sun breaking through the forest. Above the client's antique dining table with a burnished brass inlay, we installed a clean-lined modern fixture from Apparatus Studio that has great presence. We love the stylistic tension that arises when you mix antique pieces with contemporary ones. Juxtaposing the two creates an eclectic look that makes them both feel fresh and modern.

The home's bar area became a reimagined whiskey lounge. We kept the original groin vault ceiling, but we limewashed the brick to soften it, taking the ruddy red down a notch. We built all new cabinetry that is a mix of dark oak, marble and brass, and glass vitrines. The walls were then covered in horsehair wallcovering from Phillip Jeffries to suit that country-estate aesthetic. There is a hair-on-hide rug by Austin-based Kyle Bunting with a classic Greek-key motif and horsehair fringe on the ottoman by Konekt Studio—both are a nod to the equestrian theme, and the latter a place where you can put your feet up after a day in the proverbial saddle.

We performed some magic tricks in the kitchen, where the client's quick timeline made a gut remodel impossible. We took cues from the existing La Cornue range, which is arguably the best starting point one could possibly have for a European-inspired cookery. Its patinated beauty allowed us to take a few chances in zhuzhing the rest of the kitchen: we painted the original cabinets and island an ebonized, inky gloss to match the range; swapped all the existing hardware for brass; painted the white window mullions black to give them the look of old steel frames; refinished the beams; and added a new custom brass chandelier and sconces. We kept the home's original range hood but removed its metal shroud and had its exterior plastered. We even painted the beige ceramic tile backsplash a lovely ivory tone (a career first, to be sure). It was a cosmetic job only, but the results are a testament to the power of vision and revision—as is the entire home. It stands as proof that even when you can't put your hands on the underlying architecture, you can still leave a distinctive mark.

OPPOSITE: To amplify the best aspects of the home's best architecture, we echoed the arches of the entry along the back wall of the dining space, then lined the area with antiqued mirrors. The effect is an enfilade of arches that reflects natural light. The walls were hand-painted with a misty pastoral mural by Segreto Finishes, while the Apparatus Studio chandelier brings modern tension.

ENDANGERED

PREVIOUS: A groin vault ceiling in lime-washed brick establishes the mood for this lounge, where textural richness and jewel-toned drama take center stage. A Timothy Corrigan–designed hide rug by Kyle Bunting grounds the room, while a Phillip Jeffries horsehair wallcovering nods to the client's love of equestrian detail. RIGHT: Details tell a story throughout this house, from the horsehair-trimmed ottoman to the neoclassical touches. (Note the embroidered Greek keys on the leading edges of the mohair window treatments in the top left photo.) Ageless marbles and spine-out paperbacks supply a lived-in rhythm to the redesign. The handblown glass lamp in the top right photo is by U.K.-based Porta Romana.

Our goal was to freshen the architecture and lean into things that felt classic, while introducing elements from today.

If you don't believe paint can do magic tricks, look to my client's kitchen, which we completely transformed almost entirely with paint—sleight of hand with jaw-dropping results. In black with brass hardware, the dated lower cabinets now look like something from a Yorkshire estate; even the ceramic tile backsplash was repainted on-site. Suffice to say, we take our clients' timelines and budgets very seriously!

ANDREW MARTIN INTERIOR DESIGN REVIEW
AD at 100

OPPOSITE: What was once a cavernous family room now feels grounded and intimate thanks to a vast Stark Carpet tartan wool and a bespoke eight-foot-wide twig chandelier we commissioned from Paul Ferrante. A massive diptych painting by Chris Rivers conceals a TV, balancing technology with elegance. ABOVE: The original stone fireplace was softened with a whitewash and a new Tudor-style limestone mantel.

Dwelling in Light

Southern California may be more than fifteen hundred miles from Houston, but the region's iconic indoor/outdoor lifestyle is eminently suitable to Texas. For this family home, our clients longed to recreate the airy aesthetic that Californians enjoy, so we were commissioned to design the architecture and interiors to embody that vibe. To achieve their vision, we worked hard to dissolve the visual boundaries that separate the indoors from lush outdoors and all of Mother Nature's whims. Soaring ceilings were designed to maximize the effect of light emanating from custom-fabricated steel and glass windows. The fenestration was oriented to take full advantage of the home's expansive southern exposure. We also brought indoors the exterior building materials, such as large pieces of Texas limestone cladding, further dissolving the boundaries between inside and out.

All that glass can raise privacy concerns in a densely populated city like Houston, and that was the case with the property's front facade, which aligns with its street frontage. The front door is partially obscured by an olive tree that you must circumvent as you ascend stairs to pass underneath a portico sheltering the entrance. We planned around this tree so that its oblong two-tone leaves and spindly branches would provide protection from prying eyes. When even more privacy is needed, sheer draperies close over the glass front door and windows, acting as portière curtains while allowing light to flood the foyer.

For the interiors, we selected light fixtures that glow softly with reflected natural light even during the day when they're switched off. We showed our clients many different options, but they kept coming back to simple globes that were playful, casual, and adaptable. In the foyer, an etched glass chandelier from Giopato & Coombes looks like floating clouds. In the family room, we installed a piece that abstractly echoes birds sitting on a cluster of branches. Over the table in the dining room, the light installation by Volker Haug resembles swirling wind. While many of these fixtures were created by artisans and are appropriately precious, one of my favorite lighting choices here is decidedly homespun: the lights installed above the breakfast nook's banquette are inexpensive milk-glass globes from Cedar & Moss in a playful asymmetrical arrangement on a green plaster wall. The multiple globes in various sizes look a bit like droplets of dew on a leaf.

OPPOSITE: A sculptural staircase anchors the entry with sinuous plaster curves. The ceramic table's leafy arrangement hints at the home's indoor/outdoor ethos, as do the wood wall cladding and oversized custom steel windows that dissolve the boundary between the interior and exterior.

GREAT ESCAPES EUROPE

Sometimes moments of necessity lead to the most interesting designs. When my clients shared that one of them was deathly afraid of heights—including the edges of stairs—we had to get creative. Since their extensive programmatic requirements called for a two-story home with the primary suite and all additional bedrooms located upstairs, we knew that they would have to contend with their phobia daily. The solution was a floating circular stair with plaster walls extending up as an opaque handrail. This simple feature allows them to feel protected while ascending and descending the stairs—out of fear came something quite beautiful.

Thematic and materialistic elements continue throughout the home, including the use of European white oak for floors, ceilings, slatted accent walls, and trim. The clients really wanted their home to feel warm, light, and bright, with connections to nature. We explored different color tonalities in a few key areas, such as the upstairs playroom, which has a walnut tone, and in the kitchen, where the cabinets are bleached and pickled white. Our clients' favorite color is green, so we also enjoyed playing with that color in different tones and combinations throughout the home in everything from wall finishes to art and textiles.

When the clients first enlisted us, they shared that what they desired most was a family compound—a place with all the amenities for the family members to live their best lives, right on the premises. So we designed for them casual indoor and outdoor spaces to delight in and share with loved ones: separate game rooms for adults and kids, expansive outdoor spaces (pool, outdoor kitchen, and covered living areas), a home theater and gym, and an indoor bar where they enjoy serving cocktails and great conversation. The home has truly become a manifestation of all their California dreams.

RIGHT AND FOLLOWING: Soaring ceilings and southern exposure flood the living space with light. The limestone-clad fireplace mirrors exterior finishes, while layered textures—from bouclé to white oak—soften the minimalistic aesthetic. A suspended fixture, reminiscent of birds on a wire, draws the eye skyward to reinforce the height of the ceilings. Streamlined Italian seating is low-slung to encourage lingering. The kitchen's custom cabinetry continues the oak story in a bleached-out finish, with Mont Blanc quartzite countertops for beauty and functionality.

Design is the art of shaping atmosphere—where proportion, rhythm, and restraint conspire to create spaces that both calm and awaken the spirit.

A custom-designed dining table—dark, grounded, and perfectly square—seats twelve in a room wrapped in quiet drama. The slat wood wall is a serene backdrop for the visually swirling light fixtures by Volker Haug.

European white oak cabinetry and a range hood and backsplash clad in sand-hued quartzite provided a minimalist backdrop for the cozy breakfast nook, where olive-green plaster and sculptural globe fixtures enliven the banquette.

Every house needs a moody moment or two. We scrapped original plans for a gym in this room (moving it elsewhere) and installed a dazzling home bar instead. The bar itself was custom-made with Silver Wave marble in a leathered finish. Oversized ombré etched pendants lend gravity and romantic glow.

In spaces from the geometric wallpapered lounge (top left) to the custom wine alcove (bottom left and center), we designed built-ins with unusual features. Our client's minimalist and artful aesthetic inspired careful layering: not too much, not too little. Even our whimsical wall light sculpture—glass orbs arranged like bubbles (top right)—supports the home's nature-infused, kinetic energy.

LEFT, TOP: The office feels equal parts gallery and retreat. Styled with black and white *objets*, this display on the matte white oak and iron shelving balances weight, texture, and negative space. LEFT, BOTTOM AND OPPOSITE: I admit I was nervous about the clients' high-gloss, crocodile-embossed desk, but it ended up being an ideal foil for the office's subdued palette.

ART DECO
FRENCH REFRESHED
Peter Lindbergh

RIGHT: Wrapped in an exuberant mural and anchored by a custom banquette, the adult game room is unequivocally joyful and sophisticated. FOLLOWING: With a canopy of white oak and a muted plaster envelope, the primary bedroom blends warmth and restraint with elements from nature and organic textures.

ABOVE: The primary suite incorporates a wet bar where the clients brew coffee and tea. OPPOSITE: The retreat adjacent to the primary bedroom balances serenity with playfulness. The space is complete with its own television viewing area and sleek chaise lounges. FOLLOWING: The covered patio was treated as an open-air living and dining space, ideal for an athletic family that spends a lot of time outdoors.

Nods to the Nautical

Anyone who adores the idea of life on a yacht might like to know that it is possible to achieve the nautical high life on land as well. Our client's directive was to embrace the highly engineered design aesthetic that is emblematic of luxury ship interiors with all of their gleaming contours, custom detailing, and luxurious materials. The home we crafted indulges in modernism, but in a decidedly maximalist way. You can practically smell the salt air and a Mediterranean feast being prepared on the main deck.

Because this home's architectural scale is nothing short of colossal, we worked hard to bring it down to human scale by introducing elements that create a sense of intimacy and coziness. One strategy we employed was to install larger-scale furniture and fixtures, because we knew the opposite approach (many smaller elements) would only make the space feel even bigger to one's eye. We designed a floating crystal chandelier for the grand stair hall that measures five feet square by fourteen feet in height. We incorporated a gorgeous grand piano from Steinway and an eight-foot-long console from Hellman Chang as the space's main furniture pieces. Underfoot, we created a patchwork of four-by-eight-foot stone slabs of natural quartzite linked by polished stainless steel strips that help bring balance to the soaring ceilings, while also nodding to the watertight metal inlays found on the decks of our maritime inspiration. The Alex Katz paintings in the upper gallery are also monumental, so bringing all of the elements into balance with one another was crucial.

It was vital that the home's formal living room also feel cozy, so we introduced wood paneling inspired by luxury ship cabins. A rich caramel tone showcases the intricate texture and character of the oak's natural wood grain. We alternated running the grain horizontally and vertically, which added further depth to the interior's shell, and we utilized cove lighting around the perimeter to create a soft ambient glow. To take the edge off, literally, we also designed furniture with rounded edges and a

OPPOSITE: To balance the soaring volume of this foyer, we introduced elements with an equally monumental scale, including a custom crystal chandelier we designed that is six-feet wide and fourteen-feet tall. We inset stainless steel pieces between the slabs of quartzite on the floor to mimic the type of inlay seen on a luxury yacht's wooden deck.

RIGHT: From the upper gallery, the cascade of crystal glimmers like a modernist waterfall. Alex Katz paintings inject a shot of design adrenaline. FOLLOWING: We brought moody intimacy to the living room with honeyed oak walls, layered lighting, and a mélange of plush and structured furnishings. The convex mirror by Christophe Gaignon refracts the room's symmetry.

decidedly luxurious material palette of silk, velvet, and leather. When our original glass door designs felt too simple, we introduced custom screens within them for a layered effect and repeated the screens' design in partitions in the main entrance to the space. Astride it all, a telescoping mercury-glass piece bounces light around while feeling a bit like sea glass that's risen languidly from the surf, or a telescope focused out into the distance.

Custom details always add depth. In the dining room, we designed leather pulls to be affixed to the chair backs and had the bottom hems of the sheer draperies embroidered by the artisans at Holland & Sherry in a fabulous modern pattern. A gorgeous silk carpet from Marc Phillips is inset into the wood floor, bordered by more polished stainless steel. Above, a chandelier from Ochre is an abstraction of a school of fish as they slice through the water.

So many details went into carrying out this nautically inspired theme. Just as you would find on a ship, our client asked that his custom breakfast table be bolted to the floor. We then surrounded the table with a built-in leather banquette set against more oak paneling and fabulous art. Any ship's captain would feel at home in the primary bedroom, where the built-ins are very much inspired by yacht design—including an upholstered wall that is edge-lit by concealed light sources. Motorized draperies hidden within the walls unfurl at the push of a button, spilling out seemingly from nowhere. For the adjoining bathroom, we designed a light fixture with tiny lights on crystal rods to perfectly fit the skylight, so that it is illuminated by the sun during the day and by electricity in the evening.

We lavished the same focus and care on the home's other amenities, from the outdoor deck complete with kitchen, bar, pizza oven, and hibachi grill to the indoor gym, sauna, massage room, and theater. Creating this home was a joy because of the client's unwavering vision and commitment to excellence. To that, we say, "All aboard!"

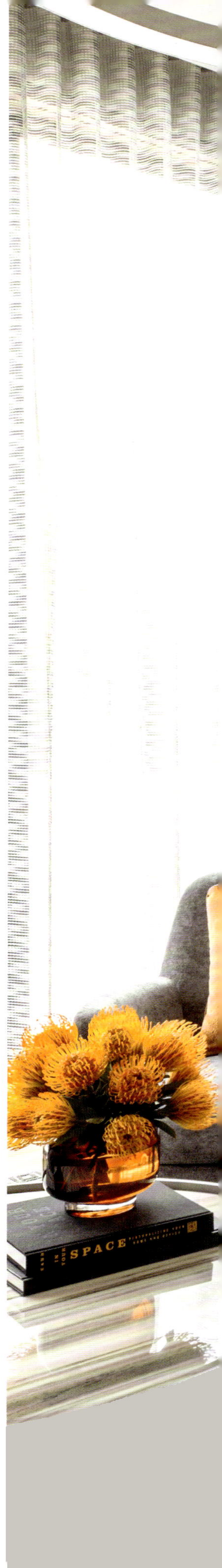

RIGHT: The artisans at Hellman Chang carved this sleek, highly engineered desk from glossy mahogany. The soft, yacht-like curves recall the homeowner's love of nautical life. FOLLOWING: In the dining room, every detail, down to the wine vault behind glass, channels modern luxury with precision and layered restraint.

BEYOND THE DOCUMENT
Peter Lindbergh

STONE
Peter Lindbergh

PREVIOUS AND RIGHT: Every material in the modern maximalist kitchen, including the three-dimensional tile backsplash and a two-toned hood we custom fabricated in blackened and stainless steel, was selected to provide layers of contrasting materials and textures while also offering a cohesive sensibility. A trio of wall-mounted glass and acrylic pieces by artist Claire Ankenman seemingly glow above the fireplace.

LOUIS VUITTON
STONE
Peter Lindbergh

ABOVE AND OPPOSITE: With pop-art exuberance, the breakfast nook brings levity to the home's engineered elegance. Pendant lights dazzle like modernist wind chimes above a corner banquette designed for family breakfasts and late-night debriefs. We introduced the wood paneling around the back of the banquette, which is perimeter-lit for a flattering glow at any hour.

Floor-to-ceiling glass walls in this lounge space overlook the garden, pool deck, and alfresco kitchen. Sculptural lighting by Ted Abramczyk floats above textural seating, while pops of red and yellow play against dove-gray upholstery.

GRAY MALIN

RIGHT: The primary bedroom suite balances layers of softness with sculptural drama. A custom upholstered wall cradles the bed, while a circular crystal chandelier brings quiet glamour. Inset stone and a graphic artwork offer a surprise punch, adhering to the home's unspoken theme of modern maximalism. FOLLOWING LEFT: For the primary bath, we collaborated with Quasar to create this cosmic crystal rod chandelier that fits perfectly within the skylight and crowns the space like a shimmering constellation. FOLLOWING RIGHT: The powder room's floating vanity sparkles in front of the window.

PALMBEACH

OPPOSITE AND RIGHT, TOP AND BOTTOM: We designed her private office using many pieces from her existing art collection to kick off the color palette. Custom cabinetry and a stunning mixed-material desk ground the space. The handblown glass light fixture from London's Cameron Design House resembles a classic pearl necklace: elegant, yet playful, and sculptural red chairs conjure a room as expressive as its occupant.

ABOVE: In the daughter's en suite bath, pattern, polish, and a bit of storybook whimsy converge in blushing tones. OPPOSITE: We love designing polished children's rooms. Here, an alcove upholstered in fluted pink panels suits a crib and can accommodate a queen bed when the child gets older.

OPPOSITE: On the pool terrace, a sinuous black sculpture by Matt Devine unfurls above a fireplace mantel clad in marble. Furniture from Holly Hunt and Link Outdoor completes the scene. ABOVE: Deep charcoals, graphic patterns, and modern furniture silhouettes keep the mood dramatic in this outdoor kitchen and bar. The kitchen is complete with a grill, side burners, pizza oven, and teppanyaki, while the bar is fully stocked with all the supplies necessary to craft the perfect cocktail.

Casual Contemporary

When our clients' employer relocated him to Houston, he and his young family needed to make the move on a very tight deadline and furnish a home for themselves at lightning speed. The real estate agent who found them their home recommended us, and against all odds, we were able to deliver. It helped that he and his wife gave us carte blanche to design the interior, handing off inspirational images along with their trust. They knew we would be moving a few mountains to achieve their goals, and they patiently stood back and let us do the work.

This project was a homecoming of sorts, because it wasn't our first time working on this house. A few years prior, we were tapped to design the interior architecture for the home's previous owners. At that time, the architectural plan had many sharp angles, so we brought in curves, softening the edges of everything from the balcony to the hand-carved handrail. We introduced arched doorways, curves in the stairwell, and coves that round above the dining room and powder room. Every space should have a good mix of straight lines and curves—a form of yin and yang that brings balance and harmony to a space. For the bar area, we designed a compound herringbone floor, but instead of running a standard herringbone pattern we joined four planks of wood together at a time to create an overscale basket weave. The existing kitchen had no upper storage, so we devised suspended wood and iron shelving that showcases serving ware, creating a moment of functional beauty. On the island, we utilized a statement stone—Patagonia quartzite—that has wonderful crystalline and opaque areas that complement the rest of the kitchen's countertops.

OPPOSITE: This vaulted foyer features floor-to-ceiling steel doors and windows and a gorgeous stone floor. The plaster walls are the same hue as the exterior stucco to visually dissolve the boundaries between indoors and outdoors. We added sheer draperies for softness, for privacy when desired, and to draw eyes up to the natural-oak plank ceiling.

Now, the opportunity to come back and design the interiors again was like a gift from the new homeowners, a chance to revisit an old friend. The wife's inspiration images were filled with soft earth tones, white plaster walls, and an eclectic mix of furnishings. The restrained color palette the couple wanted allowed us to inject brightness through art and accessories. This home already had a breathy, fresh quality and felt Mediterranean and American at once. Thankfully, that perfectly suited their chosen aesthetic with its vibe of relaxed textures, warm colors, and an inviting feel.

The challenge was a universal one: we had to make the house look and feel fantastic. The compressed time frame added another layer of difficulty, though, meaning that we had to do so quickly. We began by ordering all the custom pieces that could be completed by the looming deadline, including two-story-high sheer draperies in the foyer that would lend privacy while allowing light to flow; wallcoverings and specialty wall finishes throughout; and custom runners. We also called in favors from our coterie of friends at showrooms and galleries across the country. We spent a good portion of the budget on a collection of high-quality art. The pieces were transformative for this young couple, who pulled me aside when they finally saw their completed abode to share that they had never lived with such impactful art before, and they were amazed by the difference it made.

Knowing how hard it can be to move to a new place, we also made time for personal details. We hired a sommelier to curate a collection of wine so that the bar would be fully stocked upon their arrival. We also brought in toys and books for their young child. One of our favorite spots in their home is their child's bedroom, which proves kids' spaces don't have to be garishly colorful in order to be playful. All in all, having a chance to revisit this house was a dream—and we were thrilled to offer them a sincere "welcome home."

OPPOSITE: Ceramic lamps and vessels sit in quiet contrast to the vivid pixelated art by Don Morris, a textural field of motion that sets the tone for this cozy (yet carefully calibrated) family space. FOLLOWING: A curated mix of art and accessories leans into a California-relaxed, curve-conscious warmth that's equal parts tailored and inviting.

Venetian Villas
The Private World of Yves Saint Laurent & Pierre
Canyons and Deserts
Painters of Utah's Canyons and Deserts

The Private World

AT HOME

PREVIOUS: To distinguish the island and give the visual impression of weight, we wrapped it in thick-cut Patagonia quartzite with substantial heft. The stone's crystalline veining echoes the decidedly quiet luxury finish of the cabinets. RIGHT: Every finish in this kitchen was selected for beauty, durability, and warmth. The two-toned banquette supplies casual comfort for this young family, proof that performance and polish aren't opposites—they're tablemates.

BITES ON A BOARD
AT HOME

ROSE UNIACKE AT WORK

PREVIOUS: The bar's showstopping sculptural base and thick reverse-beveled stone top wrap downward to frame the leather paneled front. LEFT, TOP: In the lounge, suede chairs are grounded in saddle tones. LEFT, BOTTOM: A trio of floating globe pendants hover, jewelry-like, overhead. OPPOSITE: The interplay between tailored curves and handcrafted accents creates a scene that's both organic and elevated.

ROSE UNIACKE AT WORK

ABOVE: In the office, a black oak desk stands in quiet contrast to the natural oak finish on the walls and floor. The clean-lined sofa in the window nook has a worn, cozy quality. OPPOSITE: Framed nostalgia (timeworn catcher's mitts, a baseball jersey, bats, and more) is a throwback, and a great juxtaposition to the straight midcentury edges of the furniture.

West
RANCHLAND
Peter L
VANITY

Wool wallcoverings and linen draperies soften and warm a den that feels like a treehouse. The wood planked ceiling, bouclé upholstery, shag rug, and rattan-wrapped chandelier also lend a cozy vibe.

JOHN DERIAN
WORKSTEAD
HOME

RIGHT: Overlooking a sprawling live oak tree, the primary bedroom suite is another serene treehouse-like space. Art by Luke Diiorio inspired accents of rust and rose and a fanciful chandelier. FOLLOWING LEFT: Layers of texture give this guest suite a lived-in feel. FOLLOWING RIGHT: The overscale woven light fixture makes a memorable statement. A soft palette of caramel-toned woods and leather, beige grasscloth on the walls, and spruce-green linen on the slipcovered bedframe play beautifully with the antique rug.

CHRISTOPHER ONDAATJE

Across the home's bathrooms, the palette shifts but the story stays the same: spa-like solace, whether from plaster walls (top left) or an arched shower (bottom left). Even functional spaces can and should be elevated.

Within a child's room, grownups rediscover lost magic—sparks of wonder, joy, and dreams that once danced freely in their hearts. The room manifests their hopes and blessings.

OPPOSITE: This adorable child's room is playful yet sophisticated. The gabled form of the Montessori bed echoes the pattern of the Stark Carpet rug that was fabricated for the space. A mix of casual linens and grasscloth provides a beautiful backdrop for the more whimsical elements in the space.

TOYS

ABOVE: The pool serves as a visual nexus at the heart of the home, because you can see it from all of the main living areas—indoors and out. OPPOSITE: A canopy of live oaks shades the expansive lawn while softening the sleek lines of the home.

Defying Tradition

In a storied Texas enclave, Mediterranean Revival villas and neoclassical estates line leafy streets. Here, tradition is sacrosanct. This particular home stands in unapologetic defiance to all that—designed for privacy more than pageantry. Our clients' mission was to design the ultimate modern retreat: a private home that embraces tech-forward, highly engineered spaces, using natural materials selected for their raw and rare beauty.

At first glance, the house might feel pared back and simple, but when you examine the details you realize that it's dazzlingly complex. To enter, guests pass through a fortress-like brass-and-glass front door that was inspired by bank-vault doors found in Milan. The receiving area beyond it was devised for welcoming guests and nods to this couple's interest in the intersection of art and technology. The six green art pieces arranged in a grid are actually made of circuit board material, computer-printed with gold to form an abstract depiction of tree branches intersecting powerlines. This series is a perfect melding of our clients' love of nature and technology in equal measure. In the nearby powder room, we installed pendant lights made of rock crystal and brass that perfectly illuminate the stunning stone used for both the vanity and the floor.

The main living spaces unfold as serene galleries: restrained and edited, but with a distinct sense of whimsy. Our palette is simple and honest: walnut, concrete, and stone mix with metal and glass. And on the subject of stone, there are more than one hundred sixty slabs deployed throughout the house, on countertops, floors, and backsplashes—each chosen for its unique beauty. The great room is vast,

OPPOSITE: Our inspiration for this custom brass-and-glass entry door was a bank vault in Milan. It's a fittingly impressive passage into a modern architectural marvel. FOLLOWING: The architecture is the star of the show in the great room, with soaring ceilings and clerestory windows that frame views of the landscape and sky. Polished concrete floors and plaster walls reflect the abundant natural light.

Houses | Atelier AM

encompassing the dining room, main kitchen, living room, and game room. The space commanded epically scaled lighting installations to suit. In lieu of a classical fixture above the lounge, we hung thirty-one handblown glass orbs that look like full moons hovering in the air, complete with lunar craters. It's an ethereal counterbalance to the geometry of the monumental kitchen island, which bears a quartzite surface so perfectly linear that it belies its natural origins.

There are no baseboards in the house, except in wet rooms that require them (and even those sit perfectly flush with the walls). That level of craftsmanship called for absolute precision during the framing and when pouring and finishing the concrete slab. Everything had to be immaculate, and the talented craftsmen behind the magic delivered.

Still, for all its sleek minimalistic perfection, this home is deeply tactile. You feel it in the warmth of the walnut cabinetry and the silky surface of the polished concrete floors. While the public spaces are mostly neutral, the clients' wanted their private spaces to be a surprise of rich saturation. Their back kitchen is a great example: an expression of her sense of whimsy and color, with lacquered azure cabinetry and cheeky wallpaper whose pattern incorporates a variety of trompe-l'oeil china plates. (There is actually a television on that wall; we made a digital file of the wallcovering, so that when the TV is off, it blends into the background.) Her office, too, is a fantasy: her love of nature plays out in her favorite colors of cobalt blue, turquoise, and hot pink. Indeed, the room is chockablock with surprises, from the beaded and embroidered hand-painted de Gournay wallcovering to the desk—sleek and modern on one end, but ornate enough for Versailles on the other. It's quirky and fun and riveting. Just like the clients themselves.

OPPOSITE: For the dining area, we collaborated with artisans Giopato & Coombes on the fixture, one of many spectacular lighting pieces fabricated specifically for this home. The anthracite glass tabletop sits on stone and brass support legs custom-made by Gallotti&Radice. The effect is cinematically modern but serene—a recurring theme in a house that showcases materiality and uniqueness.

The lounge is a modern-day salon, complete with a custom bar wall wrapped in two-toned brass and walnut; we designed the wall, and then it was expertly fabricated by metal worker James Dawson. Overhead, a constellation of blown glass moons appear to float, lending celestial levity to the space.

From every angle, the great room unfolds like a private club. Deep, layered textures—carved stone, slubbed textiles—reveal themselves in the shifting light. Custom millwork conceals storage while celebrating artistry. Near-mathematical precision strikes a balance between cozy and commanding.

KEN FULK
VANITY FAIR 100 YEARS

For all its sleek minimalistic perfection, this home is deeply tactile. You feel it in the warmth of the walnut cabinetry and the silky surface of the polished concrete floors.

OPPOSITE: We employed one of the most incredible pieces of Mont Blanc quartzite I've ever seen in the front kitchen. Its strict parallel lines spoke directly to the clients' love of highly engineered spaces. FOLLOWING: The game room is designed like a gallery, including a wall of built-ins that frames a collection of bronze and blackened sculptures. PAGE 235: A calligraphy-like wooden light fixture by John Procario floats above the game table.

Even private spaces benefit from cinematic quality—surreal moments of richness, including surfaces and lighting pieces that are works of art. In the powder rooms (top center and bottom right), we leaned into the dark and dramatic. The sinks are made from slabs of quartzite, and the sconces are rock crystal.

ABOVE: This quiet corner marks the spot where strength and softness meet (fittingly paired with a glass of whiskey, neat). OPPOSITE: We envisioned this study as an English pub that had been cored out and beamed into this home. Amid modernist surroundings, it's a surreal standout.

RIGHT: This private office reflects the vibrant personality of its fun-loving mistress. Aesthetic touches include a hand-beaded and embroidered de Gournay wallcovering, a lacquered teal ceiling, a fantastical custom chandelier by Lindsey Adelman, and a wingback by Vladimir Kagan. We commissioned a desk from Usona that captures the riveting evolution from tradition to modernity. FOLLOWING LEFT: A closer look reveals a hand-painted door pull hidden within the flora and fauna. Fierce, modern maximalism. FOLLOWING RIGHT: The view to the exterior is reflected and amplified by the lacquered ceiling, while the curated furnishings offer the perfect spot from which to enjoy it all.

SLIM AARONS

From lacquered millwork (top left) to a motif of monkeys imbibing at cocktail hour (bottom right), every corner of the office is imbued with narrative flair and hidden Easter eggs for guests to discover. A candy-colored powder room (top right and bottom left) sits just beyond, with jewel-toned accents that carry the imaginative story through every surface. This wing of the house was designed as an escapist retreat.

The tucked-away galley kitchen channels mod glamour with cobalt-lacquered cabinets and a pink toile wallpaper studded with trompe-l'oeil china plates. It's both playful and high-functioning, with commercial-grade appliances and seamless storage. The bold palette reflects the client's directive for a bit of attitude rather than the restraint employed in the public areas.

This calming bedroom is awash in tonal blues and sea-glass greens. Grasscloth walls and layered textiles provide softness, while curated art and accessories lend gravitas. The generous expanses of glass bring nature into the room—a quiet counterpoint to the home's wilder flights of fancy.

OPPOSITE: Our client happened upon a lavender mosaic and fell in love, so we crafted her entire bathroom around it. Cool lavender cabinetry elevates this vanity to the realm of couture. RIGHT, TOP AND BOTTOM: Soft concealed lighting and integrated mirrors render the space ethereal—and it's just one of many tailored retreats in the private wing.

ABOVE: Wrapped in wood and glass, the home's minimalist exterior belies the expressive interior within. OPPOSITE: Tucked into the landscape, this garden pavilion-meets-potting shed has giant florals extending up the walls that turn the structure into an *Alice in Wonderland* surrealist moment.

Acknowledgments

This book is both a reflection and a celebration: a glimpse into the philosophies that shape our design approach and a visual journey through the spaces we've had the honor to create over the past five years. Inspired by the design books that have sparked our own imaginations, we hope these pages offer that same creative spark to others. Each project reflects not only the places we have been to and the questions we have explored, but perhaps also hints where we might be headed next.

OUR CLIENTS: There is no dream without you. Thank you for inviting us into your lives, for dreaming alongside us, and for trusting us to shape the spaces where your most treasured memories unfold. To those who graciously allowed us to feature your homes in this book: thank you. Your belief in our work is the foundation of everything we do.

BOOK TEAM: To Jill Cohen, Melissa Powell, Charles Miers, Kathleen Jayes, Doug Turshen, Steve Turner, and Kathryn O'Shea-Evans: thank you for helping shape this book into something that feels true to our work and spirit. It has been a joy to collaborate with you.

Jill Cohen, your belief in me has meant more than words can say. You champion not only great design but also the people behind it. Your friendship and vision have inspired me to dream bigger—for myself, for our work, and for the future of our team. I'm deeply grateful.

PHOTOGRAPHY & PRODUCTION TEAM: To Julie Soefer, Jessica Holtam, Claudia Casbarian, Jonathan Harris, Macy Holtam, and Michael Viviano: thank you for your artistry, your collaboration, and your ability to capture not just the beauty we designed, but the essence of home. This book wouldn't exist without your talents.

DESIGN TEAM: To all my collaborators past and present: thank you for believing in the dream and building something meaningful with me. Your creativity, talent, and care are behind everything we do.

Erich Ploog, you've been there from the beginning. Your mentorship, belief in our shared vision, and ability to see the path ahead helped shape this business into what it is today. I am endlessly grateful.

Paola Neri, I knew early on that we would do something special together. Seeing how we've grown and what we've created, has been one of my greatest joys. Thank you for your support and partnership.

Greg Roffino, I'm so glad we took a chance on each other. Your grace and humor are constant sources of inspiration. Watching you grow into the leader you are today has been an honor.

Michael Viviano, your perspective continues to push me out of my comfort zone in all the best ways. It's a gift to learn from someone who sees the world—and design—so differently. I look forward to what's ahead.

Megan Hotze, your voice and vision as our publicist have helped us tell our story with care and purpose. Thank you for championing us with wisdom, creativity, and heart. You'll always be part of this team.

DESIGN AND BUILD PARTNERS: To Thompson Custom Homes; Al Ross Luxury Homes; Erin Stetzer Homes; Southampton Group; Iraj Taghi Custom Homes; Robert Dame Designs; Sullivan, Henry, Oggero & Associates; Gordon Partners Design; Jay Baker Architects; and JD Bartell Designs: Thank you for your integrity, imagination, and pursuit of excellence. Collaboration with you is a joy.

INDUSTRY PARTNERS: To Chaddock, Fabricut, Madison Lily Rugs, Stark Carpet, Pomogranit Stone, James Dawson, Peck & Company, Joseph & Company, and Laura Rathe Fine Art: thank you for your commitment to craft and to beauty. You make the world a more beautiful place in which to live.

MY PARENTS: Mom and Dad, thank you for your endless support and sacrifices. You taught me to create opportunity, to never fear failure, and to see magic in the everyday. Your belief in me shaped who I am. I carry your lessons and your love with me always.

MY PARTNER IN EVERY SENSE: Erich, you are my ride-or-die life partner in laughter and love. Thank you for being my everything. You inspire me every day to be the best I can be and have shown me the true meaning of love and friendship. You are my joy. You are my heart. You are my home.

First published in the United States of America in 2026 by
Rizzoli International Publications, Inc.
49 West 27th Street
New York, NY 10001
www.rizzoliusa.com

Text: Benjamin Johnston with Kathryn O'Shea Evans

Photography by Julie Soefer

ART CREDITS: Page 11 © 2026 Hunt Slonem / Artists Rights Society (ARS), New York
Page 168-169 © 2026 Alex Katz / Licensed by VAGA at Artists Rights Society (ARS), NY

Publisher: Charles Miers
Senior Editor: Kathleen Jayes
Design: Doug Turshen with Steve Turner
Production Manager: Barbara Sadick
Managing Editor: Lynn Scrabis

Developed in collaboration with Jill Cohen and Associates,
at Sandow Capital, LLC dba JCA

ISBN: 978-0-8478-7634-1
Library of Congress Control Number: 2025946758

MIX
Paper | Supporting responsible forestry
FSC® C008047

Printed in China
2026 2027 2028 2029/ 10 9 8 7 6 5 4 3 2 1

The authorized representative in the EU for product safety and compliance is
Mondadori Libri S.p.A., via Gian Battista Vico 42, Milan, Italy, 20123,
www.mondadori.it

Visit us online:
Instagram: @RizzoliBooks
Facebook.com/RizzoliNewYork
Youtube.com/user/RizzoliNY